REPUBLIC SUBLIME

WINNER OF THE 2002

KENYON REVIEW PRIZE IN POETRY

REPUBLIC SUBLIME

CHRISTOPHER CESSAC

Zoo Press

Zoo Press • P.O. Box 22990 • Lincoln, Nebraska • 68542
Printed in the United States of America

Sponsored by *The Kenyon Review*
104 College Drive • Gambier, Ohio • 43022-2693

Distributed to the trade by The University of Nebraska Press
Lincoln, Nebraska • 68588 • www.nebraskapress.unl.edu

Cover design by Merriam Massey © 2003

Cover Art: *Atlas Supports the Heavens on His Shoulders*, an engraving by Bernard Picart, 1731

Library of Congress Cataloging-in-Publication Data

Cessac, Christopher.
Republic sublime : poems / by Christopher Cessac.-- 1st ed.
p. cm.
ISBN 1-932023-06-2 (alk. paper)
I. Title.
PS3603.E87 R47 2003
811'.6--dc21

2002155588

zoo015

First Edition

Acknowledgments

The author gratefully acknowledges the editors of the following publications in which these poems first appeared, sometimes in different forms:

The Antioch Review: "Monitory Letter to Thomas Merton from Belgica"; *Black Warrior Review*: from "The World We Know Is Not the World," the section entitled "Rio Grande at Noon, Rio Grande at Midnight"; *Cimarron Review*: "Letter of Appeal to Mao Zedong from the Shang Dynasty" and "Love Letter to Komachi from Kyoto"; *Cream City Review*: "History of The Ganges River Not Shown to Scale" and "In America There Is Always a Road"; *Epoch*: "Letter of Acceptance to Horace from the Sabine Farm"; *The Kenyon Review*: "Letter of Introduction to Gostan Zarian from Troia," "Letter of Resignation to Whitman," "Pastoral Letter to Lorca from Al-Andalus," "Memo to Stevens Re: Reading," and "Letter of Intent to John Berryman"; *The Larcom Review*: "The Tenth Muse Lately Sprung Up in America"; *Mid-American Review*: "Huck Finn in Cairo"; *Salt Hill*: "Letters Rogatory to J.M. Synge from Eire"; *Southwestern American Literature*: "Telegraph from the Great American Desert," "Thank You Letter to Sor Juana from New Spain," and "Red Couple on a Red Background"; *Sycamore Review*: "Letters Testamentary for Hart Crane," as a section of a longer piece entitled "Epigraphs for Monuments Not Yet Built," and an early version of "Bodies of Water, Bodies of Land," under the title "Miss Universe."

for A.J. & Joyce

Table of Contents

V.

VI.

VII.

On Cessac's *Republic Sublime*

Plato shows us that the imagination is an appropriate place to situate or suppose an ideal society. His *Republic* describes a republic of perfectibility, of social cleanliness, of balance and order. Likewise, Longinus asserts that a "sublime author" must have the "power of forming great conceptions"—conceptions, we assume, lofty enough to survive in Plato's utopia. Christopher Cessac's ambitious and learned *Republic Sublime* makes its axial irony out of a serious engagement, and pointed disagreement, with his distinguished classical forebears. For one, remember Plato's declaration that poetic inspiration is a dangerous if divine madness, and thus poets—liars, feigners, even "effeminates"—must be forever banished from the ideal social structure, or at least must be subject to censors whose charge is to "reject the bad." Longinus himself, while clearly more temperate than Plato, deemed "the pursuit of novelty" as merely a "fashionable craze of the day."

Plato intended to banish or censor the poets, but Christopher Cessac's book is nothing if not a republic of poets. In fact, most of the book's twenty-five poems are epistolary lyrics written to or inspired by the works of the likes of J. M. Synge, Hart Crane and Jaroslav Seifert. It's a literate, allusive collection that accumulates into a cultural history of poetry and conscience, indeed a republic of letters. Part of its rich originality, its ironic "novelty," derives from Cessac's revoicing of prior poets and writers.

Republic Sublime moves inside a massive chronology. Its first sinuous, multipart poem, "The World We Know Is Not the World," finds its origins among the world's waters, where Shiva "eases the crush" of the Ganges even as Huck Finn floats the Nile. And its last poem, "The Republic Sublime," stretches like a great Benton-like mural, "bare-chested, muscles flexed," where the "Gospel according to John // O'Sullivan," heavy-metal music, and the maxims of Emerson all seek to address Cessac's eventual question: "How to explain America?" In between these impressive works we find the incessant voices, the presences, and the forms of poets talking to poets talking to . . . well, Plato would explode.

How to explain America, indeed. Cessac scours this new world, finding everywhere vestiges and traces of the old ones in his reexamination of the American narrative. But where Whitman saw America as a last-chance Eden, full of hope, cleanliness, and perfectibility, Cessac writes in "Letter of Resignation to Whitman" that "the old mythologies / [have] long failed us: spiteful, racist, crude gods / fashioned in our image, then Santa Claus / as savior, the standard and poor index / of human misery, what's left of romance / and revolution reduced to youth culture / marketing strategies. . ." This "resignation" is less a gasp of despair than a purposeful withdrawal as Cessac re-signs—that is, writes over, writes atop—the great poet's fervid optimism. Cessac's brilliant admixtures of political and economic science, popular culture, and high literary allusion provide dense layers for his clearly spoken poems. Like the law itself, of which Cessac is a student, the history of poetry is the story of precedents, of prior voices stacked like opinions and poems into palimpsests. Or as he says: "The history of art in America begins / once all the highways have been paved, then repaved." The new republic is always already a belated one, proscribed by its past even as it strains, over and over, "to not begin again, but just begin."

Like Richard Hugo, Cessac makes poems out of correspondences. But his poems bear none of the random, loose qualities of typical letters. These are tight, often syllabic, intense documents that mean to trace the evolution of art, of passion, of meaning itself, through the personae and the works of other poets and writers. This is one of the many ways by which Cessac's book asserted itself among this year's contenders for the Kenyon Review Prize for Poetry. *Republic*

Sublime conveys real authority without straining; it wields sharp wit without being snide; it is sincere without the smear of self-indulgence. Indeed, there is hardly a trace here of autobiographical fact. Yet everywhere I feel the bright presence of a fine young poet, provoked, astute, amazed, and absolutely "unashamed" to be a voice among voices.

—David Baker, series judge and Poetry Editor of *The Kenyon Review*

The breadth of the problem is great, for the poet is representative.

—Emerson

No republic is more real than that of letters . . .

—Jefferson

I.

The World We Know Is Not the World

I.

History of the Ganges River Not Shown to Scale

Rarely are rivers born. No less than Shiva
offered his hair, splayed across frozen summit

as colossal pillow to ease the crush
of water—but all of this comes much later . . .

Proper abstraction requires a certain distance
of time, the oldest mountains are by no means

the highest, respect for perspective comes hard,
over years. Without a river to carry news

or wash failure, a man can lose his sense
of scale. Each night a new mythology

descends cruel as hailstones. For all our tears
a lover's hair would be pillow enough—

the earth can shrink small enough to feel
its roundness, tears can do the work of rivers.

II.
Huck Finn in Cairo

For not one night do astronomers trust
the stars alone—the world we know we know

by analogy: it's Blake's tragic romance,
The crow wished everything was black, the owl

that everything was white; a dictionary
for example of a language without a verb

to be. To live without this fear of being
loved less than we love. Along an old river

every town is the same: blizzard, mudslide,
but death just the same. Pathetic to live

so near water yet never touch it—leather,
plywood, tarmac between you and dirt

and dirt and stone between you and water;
like love, the world we know—more felt than seen.

III.
Rio Grande at Noon, Rio Grande at Midnight

Water has no memory: that is why it is so clear.
— Ramon Gomez de la Serna

Ramon, the water here forgets nothing—
shit-brown syrup of grease and ash that cleaves

at rust canyons, caustic black cough of coal
from smokestacks extending river from razor wire

to sky. We have seen the devil and he is
a cartographer—rivers as walls, the Styx

wrapped seven times around his realm; ashamed,
the Border Patrol resigns, gathers cactus

flowers for their lovers—love songs all evening
spill from round-mouthed guitars like lava, like melting

snow—a river knows its source ... Tell us
what is enough love and what is more

than enough, and what it is to dream as rivers
dream—to not just swim but be the ocean.

IV.
In America There Is Always a Road

The straightest lines on maps are the worst lies—
no one believes you but the mountains still

unnerve you, and still the rivers of Wyoming,
Shoshone, Salt and Snake, coil and curl

like water in love. The rivers of Wyoming
are in no hurry; they want to leave red dirt

valleys fresh-dressed in that deep green promise
of summer no more than any man sets out

to live alone. A bartender will swear
he knew you years ago. You can't get lost

in America—there's always a road—lonely,
drunk and falling from the Crazy Woman

Creek Saloon. Stagger. Almost turn back.
A highway can promise all but direction.

V.
Beyond Good and Evil and Idaho

Not real estate, oceans, or bodies dressed
in flesh and feathers, worlds are made of moments—

the moon, the weather, prove nothing. A face,
a touch, a word: these too are moments. Romance

is nostalgia not history; not Lewis and Clark
mapping Snake River but a daredevil's

rocket-cycle roaring into its canyon . . .
not just a touch or word but all of life.

Lives can do this: can slow to almost still,
an instant can refuse to stop being;

not a memory of it but the moment
itself . . . Without romance, nostalgia—love

alone may not be enough. Whole towns have died
for want of more. Parades dwindled to none.

VI.
Couple on a Red Background

Skies free of benzene and sulfur stench no more
than a romantic dream . . . They're not Chagall's

usual peasants—no violins, no sky
blue cows, no giant cradle of lilacs—that red

couple laid flat against a sky so red
it stays with you for years. The year floodwaters

ripped pipelines loose from the riverbed,
the petroleum-soaked San Jacinto River

caught fire, burned for hours. A refinery
town knows mercy when it sees it—laid flat

against red sky, praying for blue, but knowing
the San Jacinto has always run muddy

gray-green, the sky a constant haze, knowing
that things as they were would be enough.

VII.
Elegy, Nevada

A river explains the town. Nothing else
would bring men here—years of too much sorrow

and never enough rain. The things we fail
to do don't prove our love. Enduring decades

of doubt and grief, not rain: the last big flood
was never—few living can recall water

moving through here. Hindsight suggests a move
from pasture to desert has been too gradual

to notice. So much has been compromised,
so many transgressions are necessary

to make a world. A town needs a river
for coming home, to cross then cross again.

Irony—our only trope to have survived
the wars. Hold it like love or time or rain.

II.

letters mingle souls

—Donne

Postcard to Olympus from Athens International Airport

By just living with death, ours has been
the more honest work—to reconcile
the material and ideal (having resolved
nothing has been our only fault and grace);
to define with precision all the knowledge
we lack; if not a means to happiness,
to find at least some way to suffer less.
Not just judges, brewers and bookies but all
of us, even unemployed philosophers
need flattery, mercy, as much oxygen,
salt and sex as anyone. There is no
universal will to the Good, for this
we have too much proof. For all our actions,
for who we are, we are responsible
to all the world, but to ourselves and always
we answer for what we might have been.
. . . *Deus ex machina?* A chorus singing
the epilogue? Swords raised or tears streaming?
From here, it's lost to Mediterranean blue,
impossible to measure where sky begins.

Letters Rogatory to J.M. Synge from Eire

And why shouldn't the girls of Dublin dream
of Florida?—flowers of every color

promised them by boys too young to remember—
this stone slab turf of Ireland grows nothing

but literature. Pilgrims, witness the house
Joyce never returned to, where Wilde is not

buried, towns Beckett forgot—what town doesn't
honor men hanged for long forgotten but surely

honorable causes? And if Galway's lost
at sea, lucky Galway—relentless ocean

all day demanding what's his—there is no proof
the past is past—the very same ocean slaps

these rocks, same cold, same wet, same—days, months,
for years, you can forget to dream at all.

Pastoral Letter to Lorca from Al-Andalus

Religion, race, language, property—all
the usual reasons with all the usual

victims: whole lives colored with little more
than dirt and blood, blame and guilt, always

within august shadows of gaudy, gold-gilt
cathedrals. Miraculous, the strength to believe

in nothing but life—faith is too weak a word.
Tonight's tales of the Alhambra, those ghosts

still building Gaudi's towers, pilgrims crawling
Camino de All-Night Discos, tomorrow too

far away to believe in—all of this world
runs on romance. And what reason, reason

enough? Because the evening's warm, because
the evening's cool. Because the evening is.

Letter of Acceptance to Horace from the Sabine Farm

Let's skip the ceremony—old Julius
has been deified before and shall again.
Rome in all its glory: temples abandoned
but for those that praise the goddess Nike,
the gods Armani, Gucci. Empires like gods
always decline; who can feel nostalgia
for Marinetti's future? Let's mourn instead
forgotten Catullus and drink to Ovid
in exile, scorn those who would keep him from us.
Horace knew well: that drone of commerce and clocks
is much too loud for art. Here arbutus
grow fat with shade, subtle hills, simple house—
strive no more for more, this lesser burden
is boon enough; just far enough from Rome,
the past, the present, far enough from lovers
ex and would-be. An emperor's intimate?
A slave's son?—pray the local wine is wine
enough to leave either as drunk. The fields
still unplowed—these fields have never been plowed
and with luck or talent they never will.

Monitory Letter to Thomas Merton from Belgica

Squirreled away among the relics—splinters
of the cross, dust-dry shards of blood, profane

unpublishable love letters anonymous
to Hopkins (*All things counter, original,*

spare, strange)—head shaved, hairshirt, calluses
on our knees, Ardenne hills lit autumn orange,

drunk on Trappist beer, drunk on poems
of pious Guido Gezelle—not being a monk

but the idea—monk as sex-symbol, monk
as rockstar (*To seem the stranger lies my lot,*

my life)—faith and prayer as love, sensual
but unrequited—not worried a god exists

but worried you've been using the wrong words,
the wrong posture, language or name—worried.

Fragments of a Letter to Christopher Smart

An autobiography of reason: cricket,
rugby, job promotion, someone to dance
a slow, close waltz; it made no difference what
it was, always insanity was picked first.

. . .

No cause for alarm. Reason has a theory:
from Bethlehem to Bethnal Green's humped zebra
crossings, much of madness is nothing more
than devotion misplaced, a passion of loss;
for widows, monks and lunatics concur
nothing hurts so much as loving too much
that which doesn't move among this world—
a dead husband, a god, idea or cause . . .

. . .

Reason also has doubts: madness, perhaps,
is wanting too much from life. Ecstasy
is abstractions, groped and licked; nothing's worse
than loving only the frail, needy, living—
London's lepers, drunkards, wingtipped bankers,
the good and wise sheep of Wales, gooseberries
and blackcurrants, a proper cup of tea . . .

For reason laments a loss of romantic love.

. . .

The collected gods of all mythologies
have no answer, no means to clarify
the gulf or is it bridge between reason
and unreason—no definition outside
of politics or creed, of time or place.

. . .

For heroes must bear some blame to be tragic.
For the mind is strong and weak as water.
For thirdly London's fat pigeons strutting
High Street are not to be trusted. A blackbird,
bashful, content to dodge the rain, sheltered
by hydrangeas, seems to know. For a number
38 bus can start you on your way—
each morning begins both a pilgrimage
to reason and revolution against reason.
For Man and Earth suffer together. For having
considered reason, consider his neighbor.

Valentine for Gertrude Stein

Beginning, again. Paris is Paris is
Paris. *Continuous present is one thing*
and beginning again and again is another.
Always the place imagined, postcards, daydreams,
never the real town endured like sleet and mud;
romance not life, always the lover imagined,
rivers, cities that might have been—Paris
before the trip and Paris after the trip
is mostly forgotten . . . Is there such a thing?
—to not begin again, but just begin.

III.

In darkness we can, by an effort of
imagination, call up the brightest images . . .

—Goethe

Theory of Colors

I.
Advantages of Subjective Experiments

A world of color and shape not sense and meaning—

Nothing should be so that it cannot be made

more so. Death we expect and come to accept,

but not loneliness. *The Passionate Shepherd*

and *The Nymph's Reply*: on vacation, a last

stab at romance—but no avian madrigals,

only some grim brown beach, ocean yellow,

green and cruel as something out of Turner

. . . Exhausted, old too soon, like those odd, stoic,

middle-aged children the Flemish masters loved

to paint. What moves the mind can move, does move.

If not romance or love, at least less lonely.

II.
Effect of Light and Darkness on the Eye

As if romance requires experience be
ignored—as if each tongue dripping honey
is sure to prove a too-thin camouflage
for some bitter, unsalvageable heart . . .
The Nymph is always becoming, never
being: mopping the child's vomit, bleaching
Shepherd's sweat stains; or maybe childless, blind
drunk and throwing the money at chinchilla
fur-lined slippers; or cloistered away in habits
the color of mud, spitting prayers like venom
to slow desire; or climbing ladders, building
a nest-egg; or as experience requires, just or.

III.
Conditions of the Appearance of Color

What slim virtues language possesses lost

in translation, a move from color to word

preserves nothing useful. Each instant of sky

incalculable blues emerge, infinite color

versus no more than dozens of words for blue,

all of them wrong—turquoise, indigo, love,

pleasures, posies, kirtle, laundry, career . . .

each obscures too much—endless subtle shades

persist without and/or despite expression.

The Shepherd's sky versus The Nymph's—never

knowing what another knows: what blue, what black,

what love, what moves another's mind or how

much time together is spent in loneliness.

IV.
Worms, Insects, Fishes

Cock crows. No, just silence. The rooster muted

by murder. Every day is all of Aesop

at once—Sunrise, another wolf-bitten corpse,

some too-anxious shepherd; a knab of toads

trampled and gored by oxen; snake throats fat

with spring nestlings; claws of a raven, black

as ever and starved, poking lifeless from clumps

of reed; the stench of goose split open, emptied

of all and nothing . . . anything you choose

to love can and will be used against you.

V.
Aesthetic Influence

What shape or color—the Shepherd's mad craving

for fresh wounds from that sweet and cruel quiver?

Depict Eros as hope thrust on over-kissed

fat-cheeked newborns, as opium strip-tease seduction,

or as a wild mustang (some blond, thick-muscled

would-be god standing nearby, his sober face

mud-caked and bloodied, hung in shame, unable

to break the horse's resolve) . . . Romance? Portray

as artist: beret, ascot, moustache, the works:

defiant, striving to transcend, if only once—

refusing to accept that knowing of love

through painters or poets is foolish as judging

a horse known only from the ground, without

body on body, gauging muscle and heart.

VI.
Considerations Derived from the Evidence of Experience and History

Possess and lack. Those to be born will have

these same concerns—the pathos is always greener

on the other . . . Atlatl, battle-axe,

bullet or bomb—objects of desire change

but not desire. Our Shepherd and Nymph are no

exception. Not spiders devouring their mates

or yellow-jackets dying soon after: instinct

is nothing like desire. Older than any

idea of god or recipe for fire,

it has always been all in wanting—desire

moving through us as blood would if blood

were everything. Youth, beauty, wisdom,

convenience, pleasure, truth—objects of desire

but not desire—always there is wanting.

VII.
Concluding Observations on Terminology

Colors, objects, what we call real exists

as relationships, separation and contrast,

as balances between: craggy mountains,

casinos, gold buckles, lamb's wool, ivy-buds,

carpools, lipstick, whiskey, a thousand posies . . .

The after-image against a background of years

without language or touch: Is it a failure

of imagination—to still see love as panacea?

Happiness? No god or constitution promised

more than pursuit. Things do not die the same death:

a garden neglected by lovers too obsessed

to leave their bed versus a garden abandoned—

. . . As if a history of its effects

could be a history of the thing itself.

IV.

In America there is more space where nobody is than where anybody is. This is what makes America what it is.

—Gertrude Stein

Thank You Letter to Sor Juana from New Spain

Time measured by distance—a single road
can wind the short, slow miles from Aztec ruin
past Jesuit cathedral, U.S. factory,
painted cement walls that promise a circus,
a dance, elections, a cockfight: glimmer of new
razors, polished and sharp, a two-year old
Roundhead rooster, his white-gold mane, black tail,
the deep crimson streaks along his sides . . .

. . .

Hope, long-lasting fever of men's lives,
constant beguiler . . . poised at the still center
between joy and fear . . . Sor Juana, life
is lived for whom? Portraits, roses, faith
and fate—all those apostrophies, so little
conversation; is nothing so unreal
as communion, as communication . . .
To shape beauty that *undermines the gods'*
own golden goblets from this local mud—
Life and world as problems to overcome
. . . *unbounded confidence, abject defeat.*

. . .

The only woman in the bar will dance
with anyone for change, for free she'll tell
how Pancho Villa once came to Ojinaga,
to this cantina, how those men ran guns
to him—lazy Sundays, flat-bed wagons
loaded with girls flirting in their soft white

Easter dresses, smell of fresh soap and flowers
still in their hair, slender hands wrapped around
the straw baskets of guns and dynamite
—how wars are almost always in the hands
of pretty girls, especially a revolution.

The Tenth Muse Lately Sprung Up in America

(Letter to Anne Bradstreet)

First a new world and then always another
lies unclaimed, undefined, land or power

luring your father then your husband, seething
like addicts, dragging you with them always

further from literature, nearer your death
. . . *Living so little while we are alive*

and life is what, contemplation . . . *notion*
without reality . . . and what then becomes

of us, rude lumps of wretchedness, frail
and vain, weather-beaten and racked with pain . . .

Perhaps there can be, in this little art,
a seeming to glory—just as loom and thread,

sickle, rip-saw, claw hammer, so too with paper
and quill—*Industry hath its recompence.*

Telegraph from the Great American Desert

A sky can be too large. The land unfolds
to flat, rivers dry to shallow and rare,

trees thin from few to none. To live and die here
is to prefer or mistake endless horizon

for the coming and going of outstretched ocean.
The prairie winds will never still, the skies

can saturate with locusts in clouds thick
enough to choke a man, but romance still—

wrapped tight around each other, naked and lost
among the shocks of hard red winter wheat—

is romance. There is a sadness with romance,
and a sadness confusing distance with perspective . . .

But what other excuse? It must have been
for love ancient oceans deserted these plains.

Letters Testamentary for Hart Crane

Poetry is nothing but suicide
notes and love letters. Logos is no god
for moderns—of necessity, the beautiful
is both sublime and perfectly useless.

Letter of Intent to John Berryman

So great a need for heroes as to settle
sometimes for the mere heroic gesture.
Life, friends, is boring. Loneliness is not
a virtue. Everyone knows how to write
a story that sells: A. Goal. B. Obstacle.
C. Obstacle overcome, kisses, champagne . . .

Life, friends, is an occupation. The world's
a bestiary of leech, toady, lickspit—
men and women who make careers of failing
to understand their work. A toast: To work
and understanding, to old friends and romance
. . . *at odds wif de world & its god*

Life as conjugation, irregular: be,
was, been—the simple past: was, was, was, was . . .
A manifesto: There is no end to desire
short of death. Damn birds fly, sing, a sky
sits low, men dodge and shove, horses do
what horses do—we all have our jobs.

Memo to Stevens Re: Reading

Pennsylvania is always precisely
where one leaves it—landscape like all landscape,
too peopled, too concrete. *The doctrine of hell*

was an objection which we later got thru . . .
It is never merely a question of time:
history is to be trusted no more

than prayer, less than literature. An act
or two before a curtain poised to fall—
life tends toward a perfect imitation

of life . . . Vice-President of Accident
& Revelation *and his wife had not been*
on speaking terms for several years—beauty

is anything but truth—*we thought it better*
not to tell her. She might cause a scene . . .
Would it mean a loss of faith in metaphor?

—to hope that death is nothing like life.

Letter of Resignation to Whitman

It's all myth now—that truth was ever pure
as pure wool suits, a world green as fistfuls
of fifties and hundreds . . . The old mythologies
had long failed us: spiteful, racist, crude gods
fashioned in our image, then Santa Claus
as savior, the standard and poor index
of human misery, what's left of romance
and revolution reduced to youth culture
marketing strategies; work, spend, work, spend.
Too-frequent dislocations, pathless paths,
a *self* as foreign as rivers or mountains known
only from maps—the known earth and heavens
unmade, undone. The labors of philosophy
are always exaggerated. A short essay
on freedom and self-determination: To live
is to choose to remain alive. It's all
myth now—that love or art, sublime pursuits
or just dancing with friends, that anything
priceless has or ever could make pain
or loss, life itself, bearable—all myth.
The need remains or has been born: a world
to be made whole again, a world that might
be made—if desire alone could make it happen.

Public Letter to Robert Lowell

Romantic Puritans shooting Peacekeepers
through space, that most American heaven . . .

What we will do and what we ought to do—
Even our favorite wars need objectors.

Sparta conquered, Rome in retreat, America . . .
It's no luxury. It's not even a choice:

creating gods, reworking mythologies
as if we might give them some fresh twist

of truth. Is just to not do evil enough?
Who isn't guilty—quotidian crimes that make

a life. *Life never finishes.* Was Aquinas
or Aristotle ever enough—then progress

promised everything; it's hard not to want
to believe: who wouldn't aspire to die

one of those deaths that youth can believe in—
patriot of what can be, not was, not is.

V.

Bodies of Water, Bodies of Land

1.

Legs, lungs, hearts fail—even a man running
for his life tires, collapses. Apples

and plums
and mangoes—What are Eden's orchards if not
mocking and cruel: flowers
then fruit,
flowers . . .

2.

Screech owls sound like women crying,
wild
berries bloom early and heavy,
summer grass
is bottle-green,
corn husks are thick and tight,
breastbones of fresh-cooked turkeys are dark purple,
familiar stars flicker,
fade,
return—

these are the signs of early and long winter.

3.

A universe is never quite what it was—

expanding, collapsing, etcetera . . .

                                                            One turn
backward, a modest glance behind then white

as winter she's no more
                                            than salt.

                                                        A taste
of pomegranate
                                (a willing, knowing taste?)

one taste and always winter comes, always.

4.

Let's consider the reasons
we fall in love:

what is,
what might have been—

birds age and molt,
fruit falls,
the sun returns
but not its light.

5.

And Eve naming the birds . . .
Her throat catches
on Kentucky Warbler.

Should we prefer
the tropical,
their garish noisy preenings,

or turkey vultures,
brown as black coffee
and bald,
all want and need.

What the thrush said
is lies

as metaphor is lies—
Juliet
is not the sun,
evening is not a patient.

6.

Leave it to younger generations?
                                        —endless
pursuit of beauty; weeds stubborn as regret,
always returning . . .

                                Sad and common as men
at fifty who buy cameras, discover lakes
and wildflowers, grasping at the sanguine,
the sentimental, zooms and wide angles,
but all too often the same anxious perspective . . .

7.

Or no more posturing? The body out
of control—everything slam-dancing, slapstick
and sex, leafless, unashamed. Wisdom tastes good.

8.

A body falling toward a rotating planet.

Snow in the headlights as if a universe
were falling piece by piece.

                                        Who could be blamed
for never returning or always returning,
for pausing to look back just once, or never—
a universe still shaped like the universe.

VI.

There is no one center, and time has lost its former coherence: East and West, yesterday and tomorrow exist as a confused jumble in each one of us.

—Octavio Paz

Where, before me, are the ages that have gone?
And where, behind me, are the coming generations?

—Ch'ên Tzu-ang

Letter of Introduction to Gostan Zarian from Troia

Morning and Lesbos slowly climbing out
from fog—those *thousand ships* replaced by dozens
of boats bearing booze and frozen seafood
for dodgy hotels that buttress the Turkish coast
from Aegean to Black. This much we know:
the dead write no epics. Homer descended
from victors—poets Troy favored were slaughtered
or fled too sudden to save their songs; survivors
were few, scattered and homeless. Our world is old,
sunrise and spring are old. Only the past
feels young—a past as old and young as each
knife-stroke by men who whittle horses all day
to hawk to tourists leaving the ruins at Troy.
No one believes those gods anymore, lost
to all but the dullest of scholars, temples
long since renamed to please fresh gods or plundered
for marble scrap. . . . To equate time with hope
is to ignore the opportunity for things
to become worse. A future is young, briefly
and once—the past is always new, a past
you can hold in your hands, loosely, and carve.

Love Letter to Komachi from Kyoto

How will we atone for cruelty we've shown
those who loved us? Is it fashion or death

demands so much? Seven layers of silk
draped over seven layers of silk, a face

of chalk and paint, teeth dyed a perfect black
. . . and centuries later, what's been missed:

a few good poems, a chance or two at love,
but little else—thumb through any history:

prisons, a war, riots, a war, *The living*
go on dying / The dead increase in number . . .

Baseball and hamburgers for one hundred
more years, for one thousand centuries

and still the dead will forgive nothing. Why bother
wasting our strength on selfish aspirations

of immortality; isn't it beyond
exhausting just trying to stay alive?

. . . a slip of paper scented with orange blossom,
these simple phrases delicately brushed

with ink, just hinting desire—then waiting . . .
unconcerned, unswayable time, and waiting.

Secret Letter to Akhmatova from Leningrad

The circus changes every year but still
the circus plays. Our faith in spectacle
will not die easy. Too much has been lost
already—the history of history
will never be told. When Tolstoy found love
or faith or justice and tried to free his serfs
they all refused to budge, cautious, suspecting
some trick. A shift in perspective . . . Wearied
of motorcycle and trapeze, the circus legend
Burgrimova spent our last century
among lions swinging and acrobatic
tigers; *to tame a lion*, she said, *first*
you must become a lion. Comrade, our urges
are doomed to be no more than human urges.
Oblivion is never far. A world
to be unmade and made when there has been
nothing like it. Poems without heroes,
such is the work of any generation—
to speak at all is to speak for those
we have outlived. It was never true
that all rivers empty into the sea;
some merge into another stream, some fade
and fade until nothing. No one can own
the horizon, not even all of us.

Dead Letter to Kalhana from Srinagar

Where history begins? Consider Arachne,
the ancient, young weaver, her doomed tapestry

depicting gods as beasts, the bulls and goats
and snakes they chose to be, against those girls,

abused, abandoned—an image perfectly
unbearable . . . to grasp so much, so well;

how could Arachne not try hanging herself?
Living describes the constant love and work

it takes to turn myth back into life.
To keep a record of such efforts; the past

is owed that much. If history is art,
art is inevitable. But a past is owed

just what? Kalhana promised *saffron, iced water,*
and grapes which are rare even in heaven

are common in Kashmir . . . isolation, grief,
disappointment . . . rare in heaven? common?

There are many ways to start time: Jesus
is born, Muhammad flees Mecca, Buddha

becomes enlightened . . . *a luscious crop of grain,*
a massive glut of fruit . . . even in heaven . . .

Is one moment, for centuries, too much
to ask? Not just memory or nostalgia,

something more tangible—at least some echo
of a life lived; a wide valley as field

only and not as the battlefield it has
become or will—that much, the past owes us.

Letter of Credit to Jaroslav Seifert from Bohemia

It is not just the nightingale but smew
and corncrake too, they all can sing badly
or beautifully depending on the climate . . .
An angular picture of suffering
is the town. Despite? Because? of cold and snow,
another Spring in Prague—the world as seen
from beneath a tank barrel—King Wenceslas
did you not know that revolution is certain,
if gradual. Enough beer and sausage is not
enough. . . . How many centuries and Kafka
has not left his desk once and still he stamps
his papers and stacks them in appropriate piles . . .
After all this being told what to believe,
what is there to keep you from believing
in nothing? . . . Women shopping the new Prague
K-Mart tell stories of when they were girls—
of crowded stadiums, thousands and thousands
of children in matching blues and grays, red scarves
and smiles, twirling their flags in unison
with all the purpose and precision of an army—
who would not be impressed by such a sight?

Letter of Appeal to Mao Zedong from the Shang Dynasty

The shoulder blades of oxen, tortoise shells—
desires, fears, the thoughts of those before us,

unchanging, preserved, carved in these burnt bones . . .
Stop. Rest. A pot of wine, the moon, the good

company of some wise, long-dead poet,
the world can in no way answer our craving.

Everyday we forget too much then suffer
our way back to lessons learned before.

Desires, fears, words—these are not grounds for building
prisons, for taking lives. A pot of wine,

the moon: things of this world are meant to be
enjoyed—but thoughts we speak or never speak

are life itself; take away these and nothing
is left, not even a world for men to rule.

VII.

We all know, that, as the human body can be nourished on any food, though it were boiled grass and the broth of shoes, so the human mind can be fed any knowledge.

—Emerson

The Republic Sublime

Nothing is so false it cannot be made
to appear true—Gospel according to John

O'Sullivan: *Who, then, can doubt that our*
country is destined to be the great nation

of futurity? Mayflower as Noah's Ark
and Greenough's Washington: President Zeus,

bare-chested, muscles flexed . . . First Thanksgiving
or Wounded Knee, Melting Pot or Dred Scott,

Ellis Island or Manzanar Relocation Camp,
Trump Tower or colonias of cardboard

and tar-paper, Jay Gould and Vanderbilt
or John Henry's young victorious corpse . . .

Lazarus rising, Lilith refusing to lie
beneath Adam, the blood of Quetzalcoatl

or the beauty of a woman that was
and is a buffalo calf pale as snow . . .

Even godless we choose what not to believe.
(Wallace Stevens:) *The world has been painted;*

most modern activity is getting rid
of the paint to get at the world itself.

Groaners, Shakers, Quakers and Come-Outers,
Dunkers, Schwenkfelders and Muggletonians,

Know-Nothings, Bucktails, Mugwumps, Locofocos,
—(Frederick Jackson Turner:) *The existence*

of an area of free land, its continuous
recession, and the advance of American settlement

westward, explain American development—
United Ancient Order of Druids, Odd

Fellows, Royal Templars of Temperance,
The Knights of Pythias, Benevolent

and Protective Order of Elks, Eagles,
Lions and Rotarians: gather and sing

of *Theopolis Americana* . . . Jesus
of Illinois, that beard and stove-pipe hat,

or never telling a lie, hung from a cross
of cherry, The Boy Next Door, The Self-Made Man,

Venture Capitalist With A Heart of Gold,
—Jesus the Pioneer: Conestoga wagon,

double-bladed axe, single-shot rifle,
a good woman at his side (all calico

bonnet, bread and babies); The Great Virgin
Frontier: Jesus and family versus

entire forests, mountain ranges, plains,
and rivers; versus Seminole, Cheyenne,

Comanche, Sioux, Nez Perce . . . and versus all
America: first clears a patch of land,

calls it his own, but then notices smoke
from miles away, from someone else's chimney,

feels suddenly crowded, packs up, moves on . . .
A love of man as abstraction but not men.

(Meriwether Lewis:) *The persons who*
usually visit the entrance of this river

for the purpose of traffic or hunting I believe
are either English or Americans; the Indians

inform us that they speak the same language
with ourselves, and give us proofs of their varacity

by repeating many words of English, as musquit,
powder, shot, knife, file, damned rascal, sun of a bitch . . .

They/We—always barbarians at the gate.
Theologians will always start with death

and stumble backward, failing to explain life.
If I could tell my troubles, it may would give

my po' heart ease, If I could tell my troubles,
it may would give . . . —bluegrass, heavy metal,

whatever, the poor will still gather to sing,
for always the history of the poor

has been either sung or forgotten.
After a war, survivors always return

to the bloodiest of the battlefields
and point at *there* and *here*; their families look

and nod. Always promises of never again.
Always our calendars will lead us not

forward, but circle, cycle, seasons, a sense
of time delineated by our returnings . . .

The love of physical gratification,
the notion of bettering one's condition,

the excitement of competition, the charm
of anticipated success, are so many spurs

to urge men onward in the active professions
they have embraced, without allowing them

to deviate for an instant from the track.
(de Toqueville, *Democracy in America.*)

Puritan, work, ethics—the love of man
as abstraction but not men—what not to . . .

As if all of history's the same plot:
men escaping cities, men who abhor their neighbors,

set sail, go west, always with selfish reasons
to abolish hell or taxes—forgetful men

who die hoping their children build towns with roads,
potable water, police, convenience, art . . .

How to explain America? The nature
of things must be put with tact, *by the people*

for the people and of . . . appearances
are not to be ignored: The Christian Soldier,

The Family Farm, The Grateful Savage . . .
(Emerson:) ... *the arts, as we know them, are but*

initial. Our best praise is given to what
they aimed and promised, not to the actual result.

What not to paint? (the moral crisis of art,
of life: each act is to the exclusion of all

other possible acts)—not Jesus of Venice,
crucified gently with warm colors, warm light,

peaceful, a look almost of relief; not stark
Scandinavian Christs stiff with pain, swallowed

in black shadow and cold dark grief. Such men
could never be gods here—crude confluence

of Anacosta mud, Potomac swamp.
(Audubon:) *During a walk this afternoon*

a beautiful Mississippi Kite sailed
by me; unfortunately I had no gun.

The history of art in America begins
once all the highways have been paved, then repaved.

Notes

Section III is introduced by a quote from Charles Lock Eastlake's translation of Goethe's *Theory of Colours*. The italicized text in "Thank You Letter to Sor Juana from New Spain" is from her poems "Hope, long lasting fever of men's lives" and "Sir, in reply to your note," translated by Alan S. Trueblood. Section VI's epigraph attributed to Ch'ên Tzu-ang is from the poet's "On a Gate-Tower at Yu-Chou," and the italicized text in "Letter of Appeal to Mao Zedong" is from Li Po's "A Farewell to Secretary Shu-yün at the Hsieh T'iao Villa in Hsüan-Chou," both translated by Witter Bynner with Kiang Kang-Hu. The Paz quote introducing Section VI is from "Invention, Underdevelopment, Modernity" in *Alternating Current*, translated by Helen Lane. In "Letter of Credit to Jaroslav Seifert from Bohemia," the italicized text is from Seifert's "Opening Poem," translated by Ewald Osers. The italicized text in "Dead Letter to Kalhana from Srinigar" is from an unattributed translation of Kalhana's *Rajtarangini*, and in "Love Letter to Komachi from Kyoto" is from the play *Sekidera Komachi*, probably by Zeami, translated by Eileen Kato.

In "Memo to Stevens Re: Reading," the italicized text is from a letter by Father Arthur Hanley asserting he baptized Wallace Stevens shortly before the poet's death. The letter was later published in *Wallace Stevens Journal* (Spring 1994).